PRINCEWILL LAGANG

Women in Business: Empowering 21st Century Entrepreneurs

First published by PRINCEWILL LAGANG 2023

Copyright © 2023 by Princewill Lagang

All rights reserved. No part of this publication may be reproduced, stored or transmitted in any form or by any means, electronic, mechanical, photocopying, recording, scanning, or otherwise without written permission from the publisher. It is illegal to copy this book, post it to a website, or distribute it by any other means without permission.

Princewill Lagang asserts the moral right to be identified as the author of this work.

First edition

This book was professionally typeset on Reedsy.
Find out more at reedsy.com

Contents

1	Women in Business: Empowering 21st Century Entrepreneurs	1
2	Breaking Barriers - The Entrepreneurial Spirit	5
3	The Power of Networks and Mentorship - Forging Paths to...	8
4	Women in Leadership - Catalysts for Change	12
5	Women-Led Businesses - Fueling Global Prosperity	15
6	The Path Forward - Aspirations and Challenges	18
7	The Roadmap to Empowerment	21
8	A Vision for Tomorrow	25
9	The Unending Journey	29
10	Your Chapter	32
11	A World of Possibilities	34
12	Beyond Boundaries	37

1

Women in Business: Empowering 21st Century Entrepreneurs

The sun dipped below the horizon, casting a warm, golden hue across the skyline of a bustling metropolis. In the heart of the city, the clinking of glasses and the hum of lively conversations filled a chic rooftop lounge. The ambiance was one of sophistication, with modern glass-and-steel buildings serving as the backdrop to this gathering of women entrepreneurs.

In this chapter, we embark on a journey through the world of women in business, exploring the remarkable rise of female entrepreneurs in the 21st century and their pivotal role in shaping the global economy. We'll delve into the inspiring stories, challenges, and triumphs of these enterprising women, from startups to multinational corporations. This is a narrative of empowerment, resilience, and innovation.

Setting the Stage

The 21st century has witnessed an unprecedented transformation in the business landscape. Women entrepreneurs are no longer confined to the periphery, but have, instead, become formidable players in the entrepreneurial arena. Their roles extend far beyond traditional gender norms, and they are at the forefront of innovation and industry disruption. In a world where gender equality is increasingly valued, women in business have emerged as pioneers of change.

The increasing prominence of women in business can be attributed to several factors. Changing societal norms and values, greater access to education, and the digital revolution have all played pivotal roles in this evolution. Women have shattered the glass ceiling in industries as diverse as technology, finance, healthcare, and fashion. This chapter will explore how these factors, along with others, have created a fertile ground for the emergence of women entrepreneurs.

The Evolution of Women in Business

The history of women in business is a narrative of perseverance and tenacity. Over the decades, women have had to overcome barriers, both cultural and structural, to enter and excel in the business world. It was not until the latter half of the 20th century that significant inroads were made, opening doors for women to become entrepreneurs, executives, and leaders.

In the United States, the Women's Liberation Movement of the 1960s and 1970s marked a turning point. It fueled discussions about gender roles and rights and laid the foundation for the empowerment of women in the business world. The introduction of legislations, such as the Equal Credit Opportunity Act and the Pregnancy Discrimination Act, provided legal backing to these aspirations.

Women like Madam C.J. Walker, who built a beauty empire in the early 20th century, and Estée Lauder, who founded a cosmetics dynasty, were trailblazers. Their success stories inspired generations of women to pursue their entrepreneurial dreams.

A 21st Century Revolution

The 21st century has ushered in a new era for women in business. While challenges remain, a myriad of opportunities and support systems have arisen. Initiatives promoting diversity and inclusion, mentorship programs, and networking events specifically catered to women have multiplied. Startups led by women are receiving greater funding and investment opportunities, and the gender gap in leadership positions is slowly closing.

Technology has played a crucial role in this revolution. It has enabled women to start and scale their businesses, often from the comfort of their own homes. E-commerce platforms, social media, and digital marketing have empowered female entrepreneurs to reach a global audience and create innovative, customer-centric solutions.

Navigating Challenges

Despite the strides made, challenges persist. Gender bias, unequal access to resources, and the need to balance work and family responsibilities can create hurdles for women entrepreneurs. However, these challenges have not deterred the determined women of the 21st century. They have harnessed their creativity and resilience to overcome obstacles and build thriving businesses.

The Empowering Journey Ahead

In the chapters that follow, we will delve into the personal stories of women who have defied convention and emerged as leaders, innovators, and role models in their respective fields. We will explore the tools, strategies, and support networks that have propelled them to success.

As we navigate the world of women in business, we will be inspired by the remarkable achievements and contributions they have made to the global economy. This is a celebration of empowerment, resilience, and innovation, and it is a testament to the indomitable spirit of 21st-century women entrepreneurs.

2

Breaking Barriers - The Entrepreneurial Spirit

As dawn breaks over the cityscape, casting long shadows and bathing the world in a new light, we delve deeper into the stories of the 21st-century women entrepreneurs who have shattered barriers, overcome obstacles, and demonstrated unwavering determination. In this chapter, we will explore their entrepreneurial spirit and how they've harnessed it to create thriving businesses.

The Drive to Create

At the heart of every entrepreneur's journey lies the desire to create, innovate, and make a lasting impact. For many women in business, this drive is fueled by a deep passion for their chosen field and the determination to see their ideas come to life.

Meet Sarah, a tech-savvy engineer who founded a green energy startup. Her love for sustainability and renewable energy solutions inspired her to create a company that now leads the way in clean technology. Sarah's story is a testament to the power of passion as a driving force in entrepreneurship.

Turning Adversity into Opportunity

Many women entrepreneurs have encountered adversity in their journeys. Whether it's gender bias, financial constraints, or industry-specific challenges, they've shown remarkable resilience and the ability to turn adversity into opportunity.

Maria, a fashion designer from a small town, faced skepticism from her family when she decided to start her own clothing brand. Through hard work and determination, she transformed her small boutique into an internationally recognized fashion label, setting an example for aspiring women entrepreneurs in her community.

Embracing Risk

Entrepreneurship is inherently risky, but women entrepreneurs have displayed a willingness to take calculated risks. These risks may include leaving stable jobs, investing personal savings, or entering male-dominated industries. They do so with an unwavering belief in their vision and a commitment to seeing it through.

Sophia, a former corporate executive, left her well-paying job to establish her own consulting firm. The risk was substantial, but her firm now provides strategic advice to Fortune 500 companies. Her story serves as an example of the courage it takes to embrace uncertainty in the pursuit of one's dreams.

Resilience in the Face of Setbacks

Setbacks are part and parcel of the entrepreneurial journey, and women in business have demonstrated remarkable resilience when faced with challenges. They adapt, learn from their mistakes, and continue to move forward.

Jasmine's journey, for instance, is a testament to her resilience. She co-founded a tech startup that faced near-collapse during a funding crisis. Despite numerous challenges, she persevered, secured new investors, and led her company to become a major player in the industry.

Navigating Work-Life Balance

Balancing the demands of entrepreneurship with personal life can be particularly challenging for women, who often shoulder a disproportionate burden of domestic responsibilities. Many women entrepreneurs have found innovative ways to maintain this equilibrium while building their businesses.

Alexandra, a mother of three, started a successful online retail business. She created a flexible work environment that allowed her to be present for her family while pursuing her entrepreneurial ambitions.

The Power of Networks and Mentorship

Support systems, including networks and mentorship, have played a pivotal role in the success of women entrepreneurs. Women often reach out to one another, sharing advice and creating networks that offer vital support and encouragement.

In the next chapter, we'll explore these support systems in more detail, uncovering the role of mentorship, networking, and women's entrepreneurial associations in the growth and development of female entrepreneurs. We'll also delve into the changing landscape of venture capital and funding opportunities for women-led businesses. The 21st-century entrepreneurial spirit of women is flourishing, breaking down barriers and creating a brighter future for all.

3

The Power of Networks and Mentorship - Forging Paths to Success

In this chapter, we explore the invaluable role that networks and mentorship play in the journey of women entrepreneurs. We delve into the importance of building connections, seeking guidance, and fostering supportive communities that empower women to overcome obstacles and thrive in the world of business.

Building Strong Networks

One of the key pillars of success for women in business is the creation and maintenance of strong, diverse networks. These networks provide access to resources, opportunities, and a support system that is indispensable on the entrepreneurial path.

We meet Lara, a young entrepreneur who founded a cutting-edge tech startup. Her journey was significantly facilitated by the network she built through industry-specific events and associations. Her ability to connect with like-minded individuals provided her with the mentorship and business partnerships that led to her company's success.

Mentorship: A Guiding Light

Mentorship is a powerful tool that has helped women entrepreneurs navigate the complexities of business. Seasoned mentors offer insights, guidance, and the benefit of their experience to those who are just starting their entrepreneurial journey.

Sharon, a business veteran, became a mentor to Sarah, a young woman aiming to establish her own marketing agency. Sharon's guidance not only helped Sarah avoid common pitfalls but also opened doors to valuable business connections. Their partnership underscores the symbiotic relationship between mentors and mentees.

Women's Entrepreneurial Associations

In recent years, women's entrepreneurial associations have gained prominence as they offer tailored support and resources for women in business. These associations create an environment where women can connect, learn, and share their experiences, fostering empowerment and success.

Ella, a member of a local women's entrepreneur association, attests to the invaluable support she received from her fellow members. The association offered her opportunities for networking, skill development, and access to potential investors. Ella's story is a testament to the impact of women's entrepreneurial associations on individual and collective success.

Overcoming Funding Barriers

Access to capital has historically been a significant challenge for women entrepreneurs. However, the landscape is changing. In this chapter, we explore the initiatives and programs that aim to bridge the gender gap in funding opportunities, enabling women-led businesses to secure the capital they need to thrive.

Emily, a founder of a biotech startup, faced difficulties in securing investment. She sought funding from a venture capital firm committed to supporting women-led businesses, ultimately receiving the financial backing she needed to develop her groundbreaking technology. Emily's story illustrates the potential for positive change in the funding ecosystem for women entrepreneurs.

The Impact of Technology

The digital age has revolutionized networking and mentorship, allowing women to connect with others across the globe. We delve into how technology has expanded the opportunities for women to build their networks and access mentorship.

Maria, a single mother and entrepreneur, utilized online platforms to connect with mentors and peers. Virtual mentorship enabled her to gain guidance and grow her e-commerce business, showcasing the power of technology in facilitating meaningful connections.

Paying It Forward

Many successful women entrepreneurs, after benefiting from mentorship and networks themselves, are now paying it forward by becoming mentors and advocates for the next generation of female business leaders. We explore the ripple effect of mentorship and the importance of women entrepreneurs nurturing the talent of tomorrow.

As we continue our exploration of the world of women in business, the importance of networks and mentorship becomes increasingly evident. These support systems empower women to overcome barriers, access resources, and realize their full potential. In the next chapter, we'll delve into the evolving landscape of women in leadership positions and the positive impact it has on businesses and society as a whole.

4

Women in Leadership - Catalysts for Change

In this chapter, we delve into the evolving landscape of women in leadership positions. Women's increasing presence in top management and executive roles is transforming businesses and society. We explore the benefits of gender diversity in leadership and the ways in which women leaders are acting as catalysts for positive change.

The Changing Face of Leadership

Over the past few decades, there has been a noticeable shift in the composition of leadership teams across industries. Women have gradually ascended to leadership positions, from boardrooms to executive offices, bringing fresh perspectives and innovative approaches to leadership.

Jane, the CEO of a multinational corporation, exemplifies this change. Her inclusive leadership style and ability to foster a diverse workforce have contributed to her company's growth and success. Her story underscores the transformative power of women in leadership roles.

The Business Case for Gender Diversity

Research consistently demonstrates the advantages of gender diversity in leadership. Companies with diverse leadership teams tend to be more innovative, perform better, and have a stronger corporate reputation. We explore the compelling business case for gender diversity and the role women leaders play in driving organizational success.

Tina, a seasoned executive, was appointed as the COO of a tech startup. Under her leadership, the company experienced significant growth and increased profitability. Her success is a testament to the tangible benefits that gender diversity in leadership can bring to a business.

Shattering Stereotypes

Women leaders are challenging preconceived notions about leadership. They are breaking free from traditional stereotypes and assumptions, demonstrating that effective leadership is not tied to gender but to skills, vision, and determination.

Nina, a pioneering engineer and founder of an aerospace company, has defied gender stereotypes in a male-dominated field. Her ability to lead and inspire a diverse team is a testament to the evolving perceptions of leadership in the 21st century.

Advocating for Change

Women in leadership positions often use their influence to advocate for gender equality and inclusivity in their industries and communities. We explore the ways in which they leverage their positions to effect broader societal change.

Lisa, a prominent CEO, is an advocate for equal pay and opportunities for women in her industry. She has used her platform to raise awareness and push for policy changes that benefit women in the workforce. Lisa's story highlights the social impact that women in leadership can achieve.

Nurturing the Next Generation

Women leaders serve as role models for the next generation of aspiring female entrepreneurs and executives. We delve into the importance of mentorship and the responsibility that women in leadership positions feel to nurture and support emerging talent.

Eva, a successful tech entrepreneur, is committed to mentoring young women in her field. Her guidance and support have inspired many to pursue careers in technology and entrepreneurship. Eva's story showcases the transformative influence women leaders have on future generations.

The Path Forward

The rise of women in leadership positions is a powerful force for change, both within businesses and in society at large. In the next chapter, we will explore the impact of women-led businesses on the global economy and how the world benefits from their unique perspectives, innovation, and commitment to positive change. The presence of women in leadership is not only a testament to their abilities but also a beacon of hope for a more equitable and prosperous future.

5

Women-Led Businesses - Fueling Global Prosperity

In this chapter, we explore the impact of women-led businesses on the global economy and society as a whole. Women entrepreneurs and business leaders bring unique perspectives, innovation, and a commitment to positive change that has far-reaching implications. Their contributions are not only driving economic growth but also reshaping industries and fostering a more inclusive world.

Economic Contribution

Women-led businesses are a significant driver of economic growth. The rapid rise in female entrepreneurship is fueling job creation, innovation, and wealth generation across industries.

Sarah, the founder of a successful tech startup, created hundreds of jobs and has become a key player in the local economy. Her story illustrates the substantial economic contribution made by women-led businesses.

Fostering Innovation

Diverse leadership teams, which often include women, are catalysts for innovation. We delve into the ways in which women entrepreneurs bring fresh ideas, creativity, and a different perspective to business, sparking new innovations and solutions.

Jenna, the CEO of a biotech company, has pioneered groundbreaking research in her field. Her company's innovations have the potential to revolutionize healthcare. Jenna's story highlights the role of women-led businesses in pushing the boundaries of innovation.

Advancing Sustainable Practices

Women-led businesses are often at the forefront of sustainability and corporate responsibility. Their commitment to ethical and environmentally friendly practices contributes to a more sustainable future.

Mia, the founder of an eco-friendly fashion brand, prioritizes ethical sourcing and sustainable production methods. Her brand has set industry standards for responsible fashion practices, emphasizing the role of women-led businesses in advancing sustainability.

Enhancing Inclusivity

Women in leadership positions advocate for inclusivity in the workforce and supply chains. Their commitment to diversity and equal opportunities contributes to a more equitable business environment.

Lena, a CEO in the financial sector, champions diversity within her organization and has implemented policies to promote inclusivity. Her story highlights the positive impact of women-led businesses on creating a fair and diverse work culture.

Balancing Profit and Purpose

Women-led businesses often emphasize a balance between profit and purpose. They are driven by a desire to make a positive impact on society while generating revenue.

Emma, the founder of a social enterprise that provides educational resources to underserved communities, demonstrates the power of purpose-driven entrepreneurship. Her story showcases how women entrepreneurs can use business as a force for good.

Breaking Down Barriers

Women entrepreneurs and business leaders break down barriers and inspire others to follow in their footsteps. They challenge traditional norms and stereotypes and, in doing so, open doors for women across the globe.

Maria, a successful entrepreneur in a male-dominated industry, is a trailblazer for women in her field. Her achievements show how women-led businesses can pave the way for others to pursue their entrepreneurial dreams.

The Global Impact

The influence of women-led businesses transcends borders. Their innovations, ethical practices, and commitment to social change contribute to global prosperity.

In the final chapter of our journey through the world of women in business, we will reflect on the progress made, the challenges that remain, and the aspirations for the future. The presence and impact of women in business are not only driving economic growth but also fostering a more inclusive, innovative, and sustainable world. Their story is one of resilience, empowerment, and lasting change.

6

The Path Forward - Aspirations and Challenges

In this concluding chapter, we reflect on the progress made by women in business, acknowledge the challenges that still persist, and outline the aspirations for the future. The journey of women in business is far from over, and as we look ahead, we see a path filled with possibilities, opportunities, and a commitment to continuing the transformation.

Acknowledging Progress

The progress made by women in business over the years is remarkable. From breaking barriers to ascending to leadership roles and making significant contributions to the global economy, women entrepreneurs and business leaders have come a long way.

We celebrate the achievements of women like Maria, who have ventured into traditionally male-dominated industries, and Sarah, who built tech empires from the ground up. These stories showcase the remarkable strides made by women in business.

THE PATH FORWARD - ASPIRATIONS AND CHALLENGES

Ongoing Challenges

Despite the progress, challenges remain. Gender bias, unequal access to resources, and the need to balance work and family responsibilities persist as obstacles for many women entrepreneurs. The journey of women in business is not without its challenges.

Lisa, a successful CEO, continues to advocate for equal pay and opportunities, highlighting the enduring gender disparities in many industries. Her efforts remind us that there is work to be done to ensure fairness and equality for women in business.

Aspirations for the Future

As we look to the future, there is a collective aspiration for a more equitable, diverse, and inclusive business world. Women aspire to continue breaking down barriers, shattering stereotypes, and achieving positions of leadership and influence.

Nina, the aerospace engineer, envisions a future where women are equally represented in science and technology fields. Her dreams reflect the aspirations of many women who seek greater gender diversity in industries that have traditionally been male-dominated.

Supporting the Next Generation

Women in business understand the importance of supporting the next generation of female entrepreneurs and leaders. They aspire to serve as mentors and advocates, nurturing young talent and offering guidance to those who follow in their footsteps.

Eva, the tech entrepreneur, is committed to mentoring young women in her industry, ensuring they have the support and guidance they need to thrive.

Her dedication exemplifies the role of women in business in fostering the growth of future leaders.

Shaping a More Inclusive World

Women in business aspire to shape a more inclusive and sustainable world. Their commitment to corporate responsibility, ethical practices, and diversity and inclusivity paves the way for a better future.

Mia, the eco-friendly fashion brand founder, envisions a world where sustainable and ethical practices are the norm. Her journey illustrates the power of women in business to drive positive change on a global scale.

A Celebration of Resilience and Empowerment

The journey of women in business is a testament to resilience, empowerment, and the pursuit of one's dreams. Women entrepreneurs and leaders have shown that gender is not a barrier to success. Their stories serve as an inspiration to all, regardless of gender, to pursue their aspirations and overcome challenges.

As we conclude our exploration of women in business, we celebrate the achievements, resilience, and empowerment of women entrepreneurs and leaders. Their journey is ongoing, and their impact is far-reaching, shaping industries, fostering innovation, and contributing to a more inclusive and equitable world. The path forward is bright, and the future holds the promise of even greater opportunities for women in business.

7

The Roadmap to Empowerment

In this final chapter, we outline a roadmap to empowerment for women in business. As we've explored the journey of women entrepreneurs and leaders, it's crucial to chart a path forward, acknowledging the progress made while addressing the ongoing challenges. This roadmap serves as a guide for aspiring and current women entrepreneurs, as well as those who support their endeavors.

Promoting Education and Skill Development

Education is the foundation of empowerment. Encouraging girls and young women to pursue education in fields such as STEM (science, technology, engineering, and mathematics) is a critical first step. Scholarships, mentorship programs, and initiatives that promote education are essential in fostering the next generation of women entrepreneurs.

Encouraging Mentorship and Networking

Mentorship and networking are key drivers of success for women in business. Creating and expanding mentorship programs and support networks can help women entrepreneurs navigate challenges and access valuable guidance. Business leaders can actively participate in mentorship initiatives to pay it forward.

Advocating for Equal Opportunities

Advocacy for equal opportunities at all levels is vital. Equal pay, opportunities for leadership, and access to resources should be prioritized. Lobbying for policy changes that promote gender equality in the workplace is an essential part of this advocacy.

Fostering a Supportive Ecosystem

The business ecosystem should be inclusive and supportive. Initiatives that provide funding, incubators, and accelerators specifically for women-led businesses can help reduce the financial barriers women often face. Investors and venture capital firms should actively seek opportunities to support women entrepreneurs.

Promoting Diversity in Leadership

Diversity in leadership is crucial for innovation and success. Companies should commit to diversifying their leadership teams and ensuring an inclusive workplace culture. This can be achieved through targeted recruitment and mentoring programs.

Encouraging Ethical and Sustainable Practices

Women-led businesses can play a pivotal role in advocating for ethical and sustainable practices. Leading by example and promoting environmentally friendly and socially responsible approaches to business can contribute to a more sustainable and equitable world.

Balancing Work and Family Life

Balancing work and family life remains a challenge for many women entrepreneurs. Support for flexible work arrangements, parental leave policies, and childcare solutions can help women maintain their entrepreneurial pursuits without sacrificing family life.

Empowering Women in Male-Dominated Industries

Efforts to encourage women's participation in traditionally male-dominated industries should continue. Education and outreach programs, along with the promotion of role models and mentors, can inspire and guide women to enter these fields.

Nurturing the Entrepreneurial Spirit

The entrepreneurial spirit of women should be nurtured and celebrated. Encouraging young girls to dream big and pursue their entrepreneurial ambitions can lead to a future where women in business are the norm, not the exception.

Celebrating Success and Resilience

Women entrepreneurs and leaders should be celebrated for their achievements, resilience, and innovation. Their stories should serve as a source of inspiration for individuals of all backgrounds, demonstrating that the path to empowerment is open to anyone with determination and passion.

A Collective Effort

The roadmap to empowerment is a collective effort that involves individuals, businesses, governments, and society as a whole. By working together, we can create a world where women in business are not only empowered but also instrumental in shaping a more equitable, innovative, and prosperous future for everyone.

As we conclude this journey through the world of women in business, we recognize the challenges and aspirations that lie ahead. The path to empowerment is ongoing, and the future holds the promise of greater opportunities and equality for women entrepreneurs and leaders. It is a journey filled with hope, determination, and the potential for lasting change.

8

A Vision for Tomorrow

In this chapter, we envision a future where the empowerment of women in business has reached new heights. We paint a picture of a world where gender equality, diversity, and inclusivity are the norm, and women play a pivotal role in driving innovation, sustainable development, and economic prosperity. This chapter serves as a source of inspiration and a call to action for individuals and organizations committed to making this vision a reality.

Gender Equality as a Cornerstone

Gender equality is no longer an aspiration but a fundamental principle embraced by societies worldwide. It is ingrained in education, labor markets, and corporate boardrooms. Women and men stand on equal footing, and discrimination based on gender is a relic of the past.

Diverse Leadership in Every Industry

Every industry reflects the diversity of society. Women hold leadership positions across sectors, from technology and finance to manufacturing and healthcare. Their perspectives and insights drive innovation, fostering vibrant and forward-thinking business environments.

Women Leading the Charge in Innovation

Women are at the forefront of innovation, driving breakthroughs in science, technology, and entrepreneurship. They spearhead research, invent new technologies, and develop disruptive solutions that address the world's most pressing challenges.

Ethical and Sustainable Business Practices

Businesses led by women prioritize ethical and sustainable practices. Corporate social responsibility is not just a buzzword but a genuine commitment. Companies strive to make a positive impact on their communities and the environment.

Equal Pay and Opportunities

Equal pay for equal work is the standard. Opportunities for leadership and career advancement are accessible to all, regardless of gender. Discrimination in the workplace is met with swift action, and gender-based wage disparities are a thing of the past.

Comprehensive Support for Women Entrepreneurs

A robust ecosystem supports women entrepreneurs at every stage of their business journey. From access to capital and mentorship to networking and skill development programs, the support network is well-established, facilitating the growth of women-led businesses.

Work-Life Balance for All

Flexible work arrangements, affordable childcare options, and parental leave policies are accessible to all, ensuring that individuals can balance their professional and personal lives without compromise.

A Future of Role Models and Mentors

The world is filled with women who serve as inspirational role models and mentors for aspiring entrepreneurs and leaders. The tradition of paying it forward has become ingrained in the business community.

A Legacy of Empowerment

The legacy of women in business is one of empowerment, resilience, and achievement. Women who paved the way for future generations are celebrated for their contributions to a more equitable and prosperous world.

A Collective Vision

This vision is not the work of one person or organization but a collective effort. It is a vision that society as a whole is committed to achieving. Governments, businesses, communities, and individuals collaborate to create a better world where gender equality and women's empowerment are central principles.

Your Role in Shaping the Future

As we conclude this journey through the world of women in business, remember that the vision for tomorrow is not distant or unattainable. It is within our reach, and each one of us has a role to play. Whether you are a woman entrepreneur, a business leader, an advocate, or a supporter of women in business, your actions contribute to the realization of this vision.

In this hapter, we call on you to join the movement for women's empowerment in business and society. Together, we can create a brighter, more inclusive, and more equitable future where women's leadership and entrepreneurship are celebrated, and their contributions are central to global progress.

9

The Unending Journey

In this chapter, we recognize that the journey of women in business is a continuous, evolving, and unending process. It is a journey that transcends the confines of individual chapters and extends far beyond the pages of this book. Women in business face new challenges, celebrate new triumphs, and set their sights on new horizons. This chapter serves as a reminder that the journey continues, and the path forward is an open road of endless possibilities.

An Ever-Evolving Landscape

The world of business is dynamic, constantly shifting and transforming. New industries emerge, technologies evolve, and societal norms adapt. Women in business are not static participants but agile and adaptable leaders who navigate these changes with determination and ingenuity.

Ongoing Challenges

While significant progress has been made, challenges continue to shape the journey of women in business. Gender bias, unequal access to resources, and discrimination persist in various forms. These challenges demand ongoing attention and advocacy.

New Frontiers of Opportunity

With each passing day, women entrepreneurs and leaders identify fresh opportunities and unexplored territories. These frontiers may be in emerging markets, cutting-edge technologies, or innovative solutions to global issues. Women in business are at the forefront of identifying and seizing these opportunities.

The Next Generation

The journey of women in business also extends to the next generation. Women who have achieved success serve as role models, mentors, and advocates, nurturing the aspirations of those who follow in their footsteps. The cycle of empowerment continues with each new wave of entrepreneurs and leaders.

A Future Defined by Empowerment

The journey of women in business is a reflection of resilience, empowerment, and unceasing progress. It is a journey that shapes industries, economies, and societies. It is a journey that celebrates the power of determination, passion, and unwavering commitment to a better future.

A Call to Action

As the journey of women in business continues, we call on all individuals and organizations to join in this collective effort. It is a call to action that encourages everyone to champion gender equality, diversity, and inclusivity in the business world and beyond.

The journey is unending, and its destination is a world where women in business are celebrated for their achievements, where gender equality is a reality, and where opportunities know no boundaries. This final chapter serves as a reminder that the path forward is filled with promise and endless possibilities. The journey continues, and it is a journey of hope, empowerment, and lasting change.

10

Your Chapter

In this final chapter, we hand the pen to you, the reader. Your story, your journey, and your role in the narrative of women in business are pivotal. As we conclude this book, we invite you to reflect on your experiences, aspirations, and your part in the ongoing empowerment of women in business. This chapter is a reminder that your story is a vital thread in the tapestry of progress.

Reflecting on Your Journey

Take a moment to reflect on your own journey. Whether you are a woman in business, an advocate, a mentor, or a supporter, your experiences and actions have contributed to the broader narrative. Recognize the challenges you've overcome and the milestones you've achieved.

Aspirations and Dreams

What are your aspirations for the future, both for yourself and for women in business as a whole? Your dreams and goals are a driving force for progress. Share your vision and imagine the possibilities that lie ahead.

Your Role in Empowerment

Consider the role you play in the empowerment of women in business. Are you a mentor, an advocate, a business leader, or a supporter of women's entrepreneurial endeavors? Reflect on the impact you have made and the legacy you hope to leave.

Encouraging Others

Empowerment is not a solitary journey. It's about lifting others as you climb. Think about the ways you can encourage and support other women in their pursuit of success. What can you do to nurture the next generation of women entrepreneurs and leaders?

Joining the Movement

The journey of women in business is a collective effort, and you are an integral part of this movement. Consider how you can actively contribute to the advancement of gender equality, diversity, and inclusivity in the business world. Your voice and actions can drive meaningful change.

Your Chapter, Your Legacy

Your story, your experiences, and your commitment to women in business are chapters that continue to be written. Your legacy is the impact you make, the empowerment you foster, and the change you create. Your chapter is part of an ongoing narrative that spans generations.

As we conclude this book, we celebrate your unique story and your invaluable role in the journey of women in business. Your chapter is essential, and together, we author a narrative of empowerment, resilience, and progress. The story continues, and your contributions are central to its unfolding.

11

A World of Possibilities

In this chapter, we expand our focus to consider the broader implications of women's empowerment in business and society. We envision a world where gender equality, diversity, and inclusivity create endless possibilities for growth, innovation, and a brighter future for all. This chapter is a reminder that the empowerment of women in business is not an isolated endeavor but a catalyst for positive change in the world.

Economic Prosperity

A world where women are empowered in business is a world of economic prosperity. Diverse leadership and gender-inclusive workplaces fuel innovation, drive economic growth, and create jobs. A thriving economy benefits everyone.

Innovation and Progress

Diverse perspectives lead to innovation and progress. A world where women's voices are heard and valued is a world where solutions to complex problems are developed, industries are transformed, and societal issues are addressed with creativity and determination.

Sustainable Development

Women-led businesses prioritize ethical and sustainable practices. They drive the global shift toward a more environmentally conscious and socially responsible world, contributing to a sustainable future for the planet and its inhabitants.

A Society of Equity

A world where women in business are empowered is a society characterized by equity and fairness. Gender equality in the workplace sets a standard for inclusivity, leading to social harmony and cohesion.

Nurtured Talent

Empowerment inspires and nurtures the talent of the next generation. Aspiring women entrepreneurs and leaders see a world of opportunities and possibilities, fostering a new wave of talent that continues to shape industries, economies, and communities.

The Ripple Effect

The empowerment of women in business has a ripple effect that extends far beyond the workplace. It influences family dynamics, community development, and social norms. It creates a world where individuals of all genders are encouraged to pursue their ambitions.

Your Role in Shaping this World

Each person's role in shaping this world of possibilities is unique and significant. Whether you are a woman entrepreneur, a business leader, an advocate, or a supporter of women in business, your actions contribute to the collective progress of society.

Joining the Vision

The vision of a world of possibilities is a shared one. It is a call to action for individuals, organizations, and governments to work collectively to create an inclusive, diverse, and equitable world. Joining this vision means actively championing gender equality, diversity, and inclusivity in every facet of life.

Your Contribution to the Future

Your story, your journey, and your actions are a vital part of the narrative of women's empowerment. As we conclude this book, remember that your contributions have far-reaching implications. The possibilities you create today will shape a future where women in business play a central role in driving positive change.

As we look to the horizon of possibilities, we celebrate the empowerment of women in business and the transformative impact it has on the world. It is a world that embraces innovation, sustainability, and social progress, and it is a world filled with endless possibilities for growth and prosperity.

12

Beyond Boundaries

In this final chapter, we transcend the confines of any single narrative or story and embrace the boundless potential of women in business. We explore the limitless horizons of their contributions and the enduring legacy they create. This chapter is a reminder that the journey of women in business is boundless and extends far beyond the pages of this book, touching every corner of the world.

A Global Impact

The empowerment of women in business has a global impact. It knows no geographical boundaries. Women from diverse cultures, backgrounds, and nations contribute to a worldwide movement that is reshaping economies, societies, and industries.

Cultural Richness

Cultural diversity is a source of strength. Women in business bring a rich tapestry of traditions, experiences, and perspectives to the global stage. This diversity fosters innovation and the exchange of ideas that transcend borders.

Addressing Global Challenges

Women entrepreneurs and leaders are at the forefront of addressing global challenges. They tackle issues like climate change, poverty, healthcare, and education, leveraging their businesses as platforms for positive change on a global scale.

A Path to Equality

Gender equality is a universal goal. The empowerment of women in business is a crucial step toward achieving that goal worldwide. It serves as a beacon of hope, illustrating that progress is possible and that inclusivity benefits all.

An Enduring Legacy

The journey of women in business leaves an enduring legacy. It inspires future generations, reshapes industries, and promotes a more equitable world. This legacy is a testament to the power of determination and the pursuit of dreams.

The Power of Collaboration

The empowerment of women in business transcends borders through collaboration and shared aspirations. International partnerships, mentorship, and the exchange of knowledge create a network that extends worldwide.

Your Role in a Global Movement

As you read this chapter, remember that your role in this global movement is integral. Your actions and advocacy contribute to the universal cause of women's empowerment in business.

A Vision of Possibility

The vision of a world where women in business go beyond boundaries is a vision of possibility. It is a call to action, an invitation to embrace a world that is open, diverse, inclusive, and interconnected.

The Boundless Journey

The journey of women in business is boundless. It extends into a future where their impact knows no limits. As we conclude this book, we celebrate the unending journey of women in business and the boundless potential they bring to the world.

The horizon of possibilities is limitless, and the legacy of women in business is a story that continues to unfold, touching lives and communities worldwide. It is a boundless journey of hope, resilience, and the potential for enduring change.

Summary:

In this comprehensive book, we've explored the remarkable journey of women in business, celebrating their achievements, resilience, and impact on the global economy and society. Across twelve chapters, we've touched on key themes and experiences that define this journey.

Chapter 1 set the stage by introducing the empowerment of 21st-century women entrepreneurs.

Chapter 2 delved into the early stages of entrepreneurship, highlighting the importance of ambition and vision.

Chapter 3 emphasized the significance of networks and mentorship, illustrating how connections and guidance can propel women entrepreneurs to success.

Chapter 4 discussed the transformative role of women in leadership positions and their contribution to business success.

Chapter 5 explored how women-led businesses fuel global prosperity through economic contributions, innovation, sustainable practices, and inclusivity.

Chapter 6 looked to the future, discussing ongoing challenges, aspirations, and the legacy of empowerment.

Chapter 7 presented a roadmap to empowerment, outlining steps to support women in business.

Chapter 8 invited readers to envision a world where gender equality and diversity create endless possibilities for growth and innovation.

Chapter 9 acknowledged that the journey of women in business is an ever-evolving landscape, with ongoing challenges and new frontiers of opportunity.

Chapter 10 handed the pen to the reader, prompting reflection on their own journey, aspirations, and role in women's empowerment.

Chapter 11 envisioned a world of possibilities, where gender equality and diversity drive economic prosperity, innovation, and sustainability.

Chapter 12 transcended boundaries, celebrating the global impact of women in business, their cultural richness, and their contribution to addressing global challenges.

Throughout this book, we celebrated the empowerment, resilience, and potential of women in business, recognizing that their journey is unending, boundless, and filled with possibilities. It's a journey that shapes industries, economies, and societies and paves the way for a brighter, more inclusive future for all.

www.ingramcontent.com/pod-product-compliance
Lightning Source LLC
LaVergne TN
LVHW010438070526
838199LV00066B/6080